Why Me?
Childhood Traumas Evolved into Adult Mental Issues

IMANI REVELS - MOTEN

Why Me?
Childhood Traumas Evolved into Adult Mental Issues

IMANI REVELS - MOTEN

CoolBird
Publishing House
THE AUTHOR'S NEST
GOODWATER, AL

Why Me? Childhood Traumas Evolved into Adult Mental Issues

Imani Revels-Moten
Web: www.imanirevelsmoten.com
Email: imanirevelsmoten@gmail.com

ISBN 978-0-578-86245-3
Printed in the United States of America
Library of Congress Cataloging -in- Publication Data

Cover Design by:
J. Ward Design Studio | Ridgeland, MS
www.jwarddesignstudio.com

Published by:
CoolBird Publishing House | Goodwater, AL
www.coolbirdstudios.com

Dedication

I would like to dedicate this book to my Heavenly Father because without you I would not be here to tell my story. I would have been stuck in my depression and in the ways of this world. I thank you for keeping me, I thank you for everything! The good, the bad and the ugly because I now know that everything is and was working together for my good. You deserve all of the credit for this book and for my life.

Thank you, Lord.

To My Husband & Two Beautiful Children

You all have played a major role in the woman I am today. When I wanted to give up, you three gave me a reason to keep going and I could never repay you, but every day I wake up I will love you unconditionally.

To My Mother

I love you woman! You are the strongest woman I know and no matter what, you have always wanted nothing but the best for me and my siblings and I will love you forever and after that.

To My Sister, Brother, Aunts, Uncles, & Cousins

We have been through the storms of life and witnessed a lot, but our saying will forever be "We may not have it all together, but together we have it all." I see where my mother gets her strength from and I love all of you with all of me.

INTRODUCTION

What are Childhood Traumas?

Childhood traumas are traumatic situations a child experiences during their adolescent years. It can also happen anytime and at any age. For this book I will be sharing stories from my own life experiences. I will also reveal how my traumas started when I was a child and followed me well into my adult years. Whether it be physical, mental, or emotional abuse, we all have a testimony. The most disturbing part about childhood traumas is that some of us gain these lifelong scars at a young age. Equally disturbing is that the majority of the time the offense is from those closest to you. These traumas, if not acknowledged and dealt with in a healthy manner will affect you and how you handle your life and the relationships in your life. It is imperative that we seek healing from professionals and from spiritual leaders who are anointed by God to provide us with guidance. Counseling and therapy is a powerful resource that can help us positively address the trauma and work through those negative impacts resulting in a wholesome healing process.

I would like to start and finish this book with encouraging words because even though my childhood traumas did evolve into adult mental issues, I can now see that God never took his hands off me and this book is a testimony to that fact. I have been a victim to depression and for as long as I can remember I have experienced severe depression. To me, depression is a dark place in your mind filled with negative thoughts. Negative thoughts about your entire life, the past, the present and the future. Sometimes, we get stuck in that place mentally because it is comforting. It is comforting for us to base our lives on the things we see. It is comforting to feel like we are in control of everything in our lives. Eventually, we must come to the realization that this life we are living is not our own and that God does not want us to live without the comfort of knowing that all of our peace and faith reside in Jesus.

We are supposed to live by faith -not by what we see, but by what God's Word says. You may feel alone but, God says that He will never leave nor forsake you. You may also want to give up because you do not see how you are going to make it through your storm, but God says that He will never put more on you than you can bear. I am a living testimony that He does exactly what He says. We have to start training our minds to replace the lies of the devil with the truth of God's Word. It is time to hand our depression, our self-doubt, and our negative thoughts to someone who is capable of handling it better than our human minds will allow.

Let us begin!

FACTS:

SIX TRUTHS ON CHILDHOOD TRAUMAS

1. Childhood Traumas will affect you overtime and as an adult if you do not address and actively take steps towards healing.

2. Childhood Traumas can develop into self-destructive behavior such as misuse of drugs and alcohol, sexual acting out, and uncontrollable negative coping mechanisms to situations that trigger your inner child.

3. The risk of social and personal problems from childhood through adulthood will increase.

4. Childhood Traumas are associated with a few mental health issues such as depression, bipolar disorder, post-traumatic stress disorder (PTSD), also anxiety disorder.

5. How your parents treated you growing up is normally how you will treat your peers, partners, children, and sadly as you get older you start to treat your parents how they treated you as well.

6. It is generational!

Why Me?
Childhood Traumas Evolved into Adult Mental Issues

IMANI REVELS - MOTEN

Chapter 1

Confused by a Father's Love

Growing up you can say I had a normal life. I was raised in a two-parent household and both of my parents always made sure my siblings and I had what we needed, and for the most part what we wanted. We took family trips to Disney World many times and we always had the best holidays. Christmas time was my favorite because it felt like love was in the air -Even to this day my favorite holiday is Christmas. On the outside looking in we looked like the perfect family. Of course every family has their problems especially during the teenage years, but for the most part we did not look as if we had any serious problems. My dad was a funny dude. He was so outgoing, fun to be around, loud, and just a whole character in one. I considered him to be my best friend. What I did not know about my dad growing up was that he dealt with childhood traumas that were still haunting him as an adult.

The trauma for me started when I was five years old. He would touch me inappropriately on my private parts. At this time I am a child, and I was not educated on the areas that no one should touch...I did not understand what was going on. As I got older the sexual acts progressed from touching to actual doing. I'm not sure exactly how old I was when molestation became sex, but by the age of 10, I knew things were not normal. During this time, my mom was a member of a gospel singing group and they would go to perform at other church functions quite often. Every time she left, my dad came and got me out of my room to have sex with me. When it first started happening it would break my heart to see my mom leave because I knew what was coming behind that. Over time the more it happened the more I felt like I had to be the protector for my younger siblings. I made sure their doors were locked or I would stay up later than them so that I would know what was going on. I really grew up mentally before I was ready.

Somehow at the end of the night when everyone including myself had been sleep for some time, I would wake up to my dad opening my door and taking me to his room. It always felt like the walk of shame. I hated what he was doing, but I loved him, I was very confused. How could the man who helped make me take advantage of me in the worst way? What happened to him? Why did he think this was okay? Why him? Why me? Those questions left with no answers completely took over my childhood and majority of my adult life. Even now I replay that walk of shame and have flashbacks of what would happen. For the longest time I thought what was happening to me was a bad dream. I just could not allow myself to deal with the reality of what was really going on. My dad would always have pornography on the tv when I walked in and I remember him saying on several occasions, “I'm teaching you this for when you get a boyfriend.”

The molestation/rape lasted from the ages of five until I was 13. Looking back, I now see that during those years my sense of self was taken from me. I did not think about who or what I wanted to be when I grew up. I mentally was no longer operating as a child. I was only focusing on protecting my siblings and girl cousins that would spend the night with us while my mom was gone. While growing up my mom and I did not have a close relationship. As I have gotten older, I realized that he used that to his advantage. He never threatened me not to tell my mom, never. He knew very well the dynamics of all our relationships. His and mine, as well as my mom and mine. Ultimately, he knew telling or talking to my mom about this was not happening. And personally, even though my family had its issues I did not want to tell my mom and be the reason why our family fell apart, I just could not do it. What scared and confused me the most was how he could go right back into father and husband mode the days after like nothing had ever happened. As a child I had so many feelings, so many unanswered questions and yet I felt alone, hopeless, and ashamed.

One day right after a church function a close friend of mine brought up the subject of being touched inappropriately by family members and how happy she was that she had not dealt with that kind of pain before. Covering it up jokingly I agreed with her and sort of changed the subject because I also felt that at any moment, I was going to tell her. A few days after that conversation, I do not remember exactly what happened, but both of my parents made me mad and I remember being on punishment stuck in my room and for some reason both my mom and dad left home. So, I called my friend and told her that I was getting touched and raped by my dad. At the time of me telling her this I was mad and acting out of anger, and I did not think she was going to tell an adult. I do not now, nor did I then blame my friend for how it all unfolded. That was my cry for help- I guess...Not intentionally, but I honestly needed help and it felt good to tell somebody else instead of holding inside this secret of mine for eight years.

When my mom found out I was at practice for our church's Black History program. Sadly, I remember this day like yesterday. My mom came in and asked if I could leave practice. All that day I had a bad feeling, and something just felt off. My mom and I got inside the truck and my aunt was in the passenger seat. I remember my mom turning to me and explaining how a friend of hers called and told her that I told my friend how I was being touched by my dad. She then looked at me with hurt in her eyes and asked me if it was true. I replied, "Yes". After that we left from the church parking lot and headed to the police station. All I can really remember from that visit is them telling us that there was nothing they could do about it because it had happened a long period ago and that there was none of his DNA on me to charge him. I also remember my mom requesting that the police officer follow us home because she would kill him if we went alone. They followed us home and I did not get a chance to go inside of our home because I was instructed to stay in the car. I did not get to see my dad that night. We left our home without him and went to stay with my aunt. Later that night my mom pulled me to the side and told me how the encounter went with my dad. She told me she confronted him about the situation and told him he needed to leave from our house as soon as possible. She also told me that my dad denied molesting and raping me. Hearing her say this hurt my feelings even more because I did not want to tell in the first place because I knew it was going to break up our family.

I honestly thought I could help him and try to figure

out what happened to him because there had to be a reason for his actions. My dad was so cool and outgoing on the outside, but inside he was being controlled by his traumas. I did not know it then, but I felt it so strong. The next few days are a blur. I missed a lot of school days, but my mind was focused on him. I hardly knew anything about his childhood at the time, but I knew he vowed he would never go back to his birthplace, California. I knew that to him we were really all that he had. I want to say a week passed by and we were still staying with my aunt. I grew more and more worried about him and his mental health. One evening I was on the phone with my best friend from school and I told her I think my dad is going to hurt himself. She reassured me that it would not happen and questioned why I had those thoughts. I told her because I know we are all he has right now. A few nights later there was a knock at the door. A detective walks in, introduces himself and asks if all the kids could go to a different room for the information he was about to share. Out of nowhere I hear a loud, screeching scream that I will never forget. I do not know if it was my mom or my aunt, but I heard someone run to the bathroom and vomit. It was in that moment I knew my father was gone. My mom came in the room and lead us to the living room to give us the news that my dad committed suicide. February 10, 2008.

Memphis man kills himself during traffic stop in Oklahoma

February 11, 2008 at 9:54 PM CST - Updated July 26 at 5:26 AM

MUSKOGEE, Okla. (AP) - Authorities in eastern Oklahoma say a Memphis man shot and killed himself during a traffic stop.

McIntosh County Sheriff Terry Jones says he stopped Paul Revels for speeding early Monday morning. As he approached the man's minivan, he shot himself in the head with a pistol.

Jones says he also found a loaded 12-guage shotgun, alcohol and possible drugs in the van.

Jones says a check shows the 38-year-old Revels was married with three children.

Memphis police went to check on the welfare of the family, but no one answered the door. Jones says he's asked Memphis police to return to the family home to make sure they are safe.

Jones said he has been in law enforcement since 1994 and sheriff since 2005 but has never seen an incident like this.

"It's very unusual for someone to kill themselves during a traffic stop unless they have done something," he said. "He could have killed me last night, and I wasn't ready. Especially since I have a wife and four kids."

He took his life 18 days before my 14th birthday. I can honestly say that I have never felt a pain as bad as I did that year- since that year. The days leading up to his funeral I do not remember at all. I do not remember if I blamed myself for how everything happened or if I felt a bit of relief because I did not have to hide behind our perfect family front. But I knew mental health would be a forever passion of mine because I could never understand how a person with so much built up hurt and pain go throughout life like they are okay when they are not. However, the sad thing is that as I have gotten older, I did the exact same thing. I also hid all my hurt and pain behind a smile. On the day of his funeral, I sung "It's So Hard to Say Goodbye to Yesterday" by Boyz II Men.

Confusing?

Right.

But, before my dad left this earth, the way he lived taught me to live in my truth. Yes, my dad raped me and took my innocence before I even knew what it was, but I still loved him as a person. I knew even at my youngest age that my dad been through some bad things in his life and I have never been afraid to show my love for him during and after death.

To My Father,

The words I never got to say before you left, I would like to say them now. I forgive you; I forgive you for taking something so precious from me and using it to your advantage. I forgive you for not stopping and letting it last for years. And I forgive you for lying about it. Now that I am older and I see from my own experience how your childhood traumas affected your parenting and personal life, I understand. The part that is hard for me to understand is why you never got the help you desperately needed for yourself, your wife, and your kids. We needed the healthy version of you then and we need it now. But I love you and I will always love you and I promise to talk about mental health, depression, and suicide until the day I leave this earth.

Love Imani

Chapter 2

Emotionally Unavailable

When and where do we learn how to properly exercise and control our emotions? Naturally during our childhood and adolescent years and normally from our parents, grandparents, etc., but unfortunately many people have to reteach themselves the correct way to use emotions once they become an adult. By then it is hard to unlearn what you have already been taught. Now I know you guys are wondering how this went on for eight years without me telling my mom or without her noticing a difference in me to figure it out. Well, like I mentioned before me and my mother were not close. When I think back, I do not remember us having any type of relationship at all. Don't get me wrong my mother was very much present in our lives and she most certainly worked hard to make sure we had everything we needed and sometimes what we wanted. My mom was and still is an active Christian, she had us in church every Sunday and bible study every Wednesday. Even after my dad's passing it still seemed as if we were a family with few issues, but behind closed doors, we were so broken. As a child I only viewed my mother as a provider, because she did not talk to us about life or anything other than no boyfriend, no sex, and go to school. With that being the dynamic of our relationship, I felt alone a lot. I did not tell my mother honestly because I did not think she would believe or protect me. My mom was strict and strong minded about a lot of things and she made it extremely hard to talk to her about anything, especially me being touched and raped by my dad, her husband. Like I mentioned before, my dad knew how my mother and my relationship was which is why he never suspected that I would talk to her about it. So, if being taken advantage of by my own blood was not traumatizing enough, having to handle my thoughts, emotions, and feelings on my own made it 10 times worse.

Growing up the only thing I knew about my parent's childhood is that my mom lost her mom when she was just 12 and was then raised by my granddad and my dad was raised by his father where he occasionally got beaten sometimes for things he did not do. I also learned that they both served time in the military and that is actually how they met. Being raised by two people who also experienced traumas and have been trained to be strong willed, strong minded and strict had its moments. Just like most families we were disciplined when we did wrong or showed any type of disrespect. And now that I am a parent I completely agree with discipline when it's needed because it is showing direction for kids as far as what is wrong and what is right. But sometimes parents can take it too far and it is no longer considered discipline, but rather physical abuse.

I experienced this type of abuse as a child and teenager growing up on top of the emotional and sexual abuse that was already attached to me. I know in the black community especially, it is common that you hear stories of grandma or "Big momma" using shoes, brooms, extension cords and etc. to beat or as they put it, discipline a child. However, that does not excuse the fact that this type of discipline with no explanation can be damaging to a child. It may get them in line at that moment, but it also places fear and anger inside of them for the future. This is why a lot of my generation do not know how to handle disagreements with partner's, family, and friends without taking things the wrong way and getting angry first before trying to understand. My dad did not like for us to have C's on our report cards, and I remember one year in elementary that C's were all I mainly had. This was also around the time when we had to get our report cards signed and brought back to school so the teacher can make sure that the parent saw it. So, my genius self decides to trace over all of the C's and turn them into B's with a pencil so that I can go back and erase it once I got the signature. Well, let us just say my dad was far from slow, but the way he disciplined me was like he was taking his anger out on me. He grabbed the paddle that he used frequently to discipline us and hit me with that paddle until it broke. He then proceeded to get a belt and he whopped me with a belt until my mom said it was enough. I will never forget how black and blue my legs, thighs and butt were. I could not sit down or lay on my back for a week. That was the kind of physical abuse that instilled anger in me.

A few years after my dad's passing, we moved into a new home. My mom not only wanted a new scenery, but she also wanted to take me away from the place where everything happened. As you can imagine life for my family, and I were not the same. It was now just my mom, brother, sister, and me. For the longest time I wanted to take my own life because I felt like our new reality was my fault. We would not have been here if I would have not said anything... But nothing I could think or say would change our new life. I was entering into my teenage years or as the old folk call it "smelling yourself years". I definitely had my "I'm grown, and I don't care what my mom says" moments, but a lot of my attitude stemmed from anger and hurt, because I felt alone all of those years. Honestly, I did not respect my mother's authority and it showed. It was not verbal disrespect that she mainly got from me, even though I did get smart mouth with her often. I just did what I wanted to do when it came to my clothes, boys, and curfews. I made my own decisions and cared less about what my mom thought. With me being the oldest, my siblings, especially my sister followed in my footsteps when it came to disrespect and doing what she wanted to do. My mother's relationship with all of us were the same when it came to discipline. We viewed her then as a "Because I said so" mom. It did not matter what we wanted to do or what we wanted- if my mom said no that was it, no explanation period just because I said so. That also made me more curious and rebellious. I could not open up to her about serious things that were going on in my life and she was far from patient and understanding with me and my feelings.

Chapter 3

You Can Leave

One evening, I can't remember if I was in the 11th or 12th grade, but my siblings and I made my mom very mad about something. I do not remember exactly what we did, but I know she was mad because she made my siblings and I sit in the garage, it was let up of course, but we had to sit in there all evening until it was time for us to go to bed. We could not have our electronics or leave the garage, we could only come in the house to use the restroom and eat, and back outside in the garage we had to go. Me, being the rebellious, angry teenager I was, went in the house, grabbed the house phone walked back outside and proceeded to call a friend while my mom was still in the house. My mom came outside, saw that I was on the phone and demanded that I hang up. I replied in a smart mouth way and it escalated from that point. She charged at me like she was going to tackle me. That was the first time my mother and I got into a physical fight. It ended with her holding a brick over my head and yelling that she brought me into this world, and she can take me out. She told me to go upstairs and pack a garbage bag with my things so I that I could get out of her house. But, since she paid for everything I had, she changed her mind and told me to get in the car with what I had on my back. One sock, no shoes, one contact lens a shirt and pants. My mom dropped me off at a gas station and left. I sat down and cried as people walked past asking if I needed help or to use a phone. A few moments later my aunt came, I figured my mom called her, but she picked me up and took me to her house until the next day when things cooled down. I can’t tell you how many times I have felt completely alone and misunderstood during my childhood and teenage life. That night was the worst night of my teenage experience because I felt like thrown out trash. I loved my mom regardless of all the things she had and had not done. I was just acting as a hurt child dealing with childhood traumas on my own.

When a Child Cries

I’m not talking about the cry from a child who has just fallen off his bike, or the cry from a child who just lost their favorite toy,
I’m talking about the silent cries,
The cries no one hears on the outside, but it’s nonstop in our ears,
The internal cries that we as confused, hurt kids keep silent for the sake of others,
The cry we train ourselves everyday not to show, but don’t know how to handle so it comes off as rebellion,
See what you see is a child that don’t want to listen “smelling themselves” as the old folk say,
What the child sees is you not wanting to listen, not being there to listen or not caring enough to do either,
You are the adult,
We are the children,
We shouldn't have to cry silent cries like we have no one,
We shouldn't have to keep secrets because adults haven't healed from their traumas, so they then in return give us their traumas before real life gets a chance,
We are the children,

We shouldn't have to cry silent cries like we don’t have any parents,

Parents as in the two people God placed on this earth to love and show us how to love unconditionally,

Parents as in the people we did not ask to be here,

but they sometimes make us feel like irritations,

We shouldn't have to step into the adult mindset as kids because you as the adult can’t handle your responsibilities,

We are the children,

And when we cry sometimes it shows as rebellion, but sometimes it’s because we are crying SILENT CRIES,

Just listen!

Chapter 4

Life Before Healing

Just Enough? Men and women, have you ever stayed in a relationship where they gave you just enough? Just enough love to make you stay. Just enough love to make you feel like this is as good as it is going to get. Just enough love to make you crazy. Well, I have had my fair share of just enough. When you grow up and the word love is associated with pain and distance, you naturally gravitate towards relationships that include pain and distance. I was confused by what love should look like, just enough was more than enough for me. During my high school and the beginning of my college years, I had a one-track mind towards everyone, males in general. I never trusted men and sex with no emotions attached was so easy and kind of fun for me to do. Like I said before, after my dad's passing, I became rebellious. From sneaking out the house with boys, sneaking boys in the house and skipping school, I did it all. I only felt comfortable around guys my age and I had bad anxiety around older men. But along the way I also dealt with other grown men attempting (not succeeding) to take advantage of me including a professor at my college. I had never had any interaction with him other than turning in assignments and attending his class. But one day at the end of the semester when we had gotten our final grades there was an incident where he told me to come to his office to speak about my grade, which was a C, not a failing grade so I was confused, but curious if he wanted to help me boost my grade as my professor... I was not thinking anything otherwise. Once I got there, like always when something seems wrong, I started to have an off feeling.

The conversation started with, "We are here to talk about your grade...You can give me head for a B or have sex with me for an A". I noticed that my dad also took something from me all those years ago, my ability to speak up for myself against adults. I told the professor in a calm manner I would go and come back. I found myself running out of that building crying as I called my mom. She instantly drove to the college to confront the professor, but we talked with the Dean and they assured us that the professor would be fired, and I never saw him again after that day.

Chapter 5

Then I Met Him

It was not until my sophomore year of college that I met someone who made me rethink the way I felt about relationships. My now husband. The first day I saw him I knew he was going to be mine. We met in trigonometry class and it is funny because he caught my attention by not paying attention. While the teacher was calling roll, he had his earphones in his ear, and everyone turned to look at him because he was the only one that had not answered. So, he basically brought his self to my attention lol. The next day he was in my apartment, not for me lol, but one of my best friends knew his best friend and he was with him when they stopped by. I clearly thought that was a sign. You can say after that day we were inseparable. By the time we committed to a relationship he had me in love with him. I actually told myself that with him I was going to be completely transparent, honest, and faithful no matter what, and I did. That is how I knew something was different because I never felt like I wanted to be with one person so much in my life. He became my world and I attached myself to him.

What made me fall even more in love with him was that he planned my 21st birthday with my closest friends- They took me to Atlanta to celebrate. He surprised me by driving to Atlanta by himself to be there with me. No one I ever dated made me feel as special as he did that weekend. I even made an Instagram post declaring him to be my husband that weekend. Our relationship took a turn for the worst when I found out that he was still communicating with his ex-girlfriend. From the time I found out about that, well into our married years, I held a grudge towards him and my thoughts and attitude towards him proved that. I wish I knew then what I know now. At the time Cortland and I got together I did not know that a few months prior he lost his own best friend, his grandmother. He was not mentally prepared for a serious relationship at that time like he said he was, like I wanted. To be honest, I was not mentally prepared either, because I had not healed from the pains of my past. I stayed because I was accustomed to that feeling and like women who have been abused before we become protectors, constantly trying to prove our loyalty, and wanting to love our men through their issues even if that means taking a back seat to our own. But because he showed me "just enough" I stayed through multiple instances where we probably should have gone our separate ways.

While wanting to prove myself loyal to him, I lost myself even more. I became even more angry, with an awfully bad attitude towards him especially when I suspected he was doing anything. I had no self-esteem and extraordinarily little love for myself. But somehow, we always bounced back from the bull-crap. Even though there was deception and a lot of side-neck talking (on my part) in our relationship I knew he would do anything for me, and he knew that I genuinely cared about him. So, at the end of the day nothing else mattered. Seven months into our relationship we moved into our first apartment together. Both of our mothers were totally against this move because we were so young and still in school. But of course, like the rebellious individuals we were, we did it anyway. I loved him so much because he never verbally or physically disrespected me, and the way he took care of me and our responsibilities was grown man status. It was all new to me being with someone who handled business the way he did without complaining or being upset about doing it. He was not the most-wealthy man, but then and even now he has never made me feel bad because he pays or had paid for everything at times. Ever since I met him, he has always said "Don't worry about a job, I got you" and he has always stood by those words.

I feel strongly about following rules on a job that don't align with what is morally right and fair, so I have always expressed that in order for me to stay employed at a company I would have to be passionate about it and love every part of my job. He always understood that and never made me feel bad for my choices.

Chapter 6

First Comes Baby...Then Comes Marriage

By July 2015, I found out I was pregnant with my first child at the age of 21. Boy was I in for a rude awakening. You see at this point I did not know how to love myself or anyone else. Like everyone else I wanted to look like or make it appear as if I had it all together. Let's get into how not only it is hard, but also destructive during pregnancy and after to have children before you heal from your past and childhood traumas. This subject has been passed down for generations. It is normal, especially in today's society, to have a relationship before friendship, sex before actually knowing your partner and babies before marriage. This is a destructive cycle we must break in order to see a change in the generations to come, we must be that example for our kids.

I did not realize how fast and how rushed my husband and my life was until I started writing this book. Because the next month on August 30, 2015 to be exact, my best friend asked me to marry him. I said yes, of course! This was a very emotional day for me because, after being used most of my life I really never thought I would be valuable enough to be someone's wife, especially not at the age of 21.

Once the high of that special day came down, I, still being stuck mentally in my traumas began to think about all of the negatives that could come out of something that is supposed to be good. I began to second guess everything. Is he wanting to marry me just because we have a baby on the way? Was he pressured into this decision? Why me? I even asked him those same questions and he reassured me that this was genuine, even till this day I will still ask to make sure his answer is the same. In that moment I really just wanted to make it clear for my own sanity that getting married just because we have a baby is not something I wanted to do. Of course, I wanted the feeling of being a family and having someone to call mine, but if the feelings were not genuine, I could do without the extra stress of adding marriage in our lives. I knew though, he was doing what he thought was best for the family we just created. That was just enough for me.

March 22, 2016, we welcomed our beautiful 7lb and 13oz, baby girl Za'Kiyah Jeanae Moten into this world. I thought my life had changed drastically before, but motherhood was another level of change, it was not about just me anymore. I was now officially responsible for another life.

Now by this time I would say, since the beginning of my college years, my mother and my relationship was progressing. I began talking to her about any and everything that I was dealing with and she did not judge or belittle me. She was the only parent I had, and I just wanted to forget the feelings of our past and move forward without addressing anything. During and after I gave birth my mother was by my side. She even stayed to help us for a month after having my daughter. I honestly do not know what I would have done without her because as soon as we left the hospital I was hit with a wave of different emotions. I would cry out of nowhere, and I would get irritated when I did not know why my baby was crying hysterically especially if she was changed, fed and burped. I later learned that I was dealing with postpartum depression. I already had regular depression, but going from worrying only about myself, to now worrying about the life of someone so tiny made my depression 10 times worse.

I noticed I had a real problem loving someone emotionally when I had my daughter...I knew without a doubt that I loved her unconditionally. I mean I will go to war with anyone about her and she never left my side, but I did not emotionally feel like a mother and some days I still do not. Keep in mind that I had just gotten engaged and just gave birth to my daughter. So, not only was I learning how to be a new mom, but I was also planning a wedding, going to marriage counseling, in college, a

Biology major to be exact, and preparing to be a new wife all at the same time.

All at age 22.

It was a mental disaster.

Life before healing is a repetitive cycle of negative thoughts, self-destructive behavior, and feeling like it is me vs. everyone. Trust me when I say that just because you have a baby or get married, it will not wash your past away or make your life better. If anything, it makes it a thousand times harder. I thought that when I had my baby, I would finally feel unconditional love. Well, that's exactly what I got. I knew my baby loved me unconditionally, but it was my job to make her feel loved unconditionally. How could I do that when I did not love myself that way. It took me a long time to feel like a mom, but I had no choice, she needed me and after seeing her face I knew I needed her.

Cortland and I set our date. July 9, 2016 would be the day our worlds officially intertwined. I had a vision for everything; the colors would be red and turquoise, my daughter would come in on a carriage with a sign that says "Daddy, it's too late to run, cause here mommy comes", and overall, it would be a fairytale setting. During the planning process I wanted my grandfather (my dad's father) to walk me down the aisle. I spoke with him about it because growing up we talked to my grandfather a lot, even though he stayed in California and we stayed in Memphis, he was ecstatic and happy to walk his granddaughter down the aisle to her future husband. Little did I know that just a few months before my wedding, my grandfather would also commit suicide the same way my father did.

Suspect in deadly shooting rampage kills himself when police attempt arrest John Revels, who was being sought in the shooting deaths of two people and the wounding of two others in the L.A. area, shot himself as CHP officers were preparing to take him into custody Friday along Interstate 15.
(Hawthorne Police)
By RICHARD WINTONSTAFF WRITER
NOV. 14, 2015
5:49 PM
The suspect in a day-long shooting rampage in the Los Angeles area that left two dead and two wounded took his own life as California Highway Patrol officers attempted to arrest him Friday near Barstow, authorities said.

John Revels, 64, shot himself on the side of Interstate 15 Friday afternoon after a series of shootings where he targeted people he knew, took the life of his live-in girlfriend and left his brother gravely wounded, said Lt. Aimee Yoshida of the Hawthorne Police Department. The deadly events began to unfold Thursday when Hawthorne police responded to a report of a shooting involving a suspect later identified as Revels in the 12900 block of Doty Avenue about 4 p.m. Thursday, Yoshida said. Two people were found shot inside the home.

The victims were taken to a local hospital, where one male victim later died from a gunshot wound to the head. He was determined to be brain dead Friday and later removed from life support. The other man suffered a gunshot wound to the arm and remains in the hospital. Revels was seen leaving the scene of the shooting, and police notified other local law enforcement agencies to be on the alert for his gold-colored Jaguar.

About an hour and a half later, a man believed to be Revels' brother was shot in the 1600 block of West 36th Place in South Los Angeles, Los Angeles police said. Detectives notified Hawthorne police after they discovered that the gunman's vehicle matched the description of the vehicle in the Hawthorne double shooting.

The wounded man was taken to a hospital and remains in critical but grave condition, Yoshida said. "At that point, we knew he shot at least two in Hawthorne-- people he knew and his brother, so agencies were searching for him across California," she said

As the manhunt widened, Hawthorne detectives learned that Revels may have fled to Las Vegas. "We know he knew people in Vegas. We haven't found anything there yet," Yoshida said. But detectives later learned that he was returning to L.A. on Interstate 15.

A CHP patrol car spotted Revels' Jaguar on Friday afternoon with a flat tire parked alongside the southbound 15 Freeway near Ghost Town Road just north of Barstow, authorities said. When back-up officers arrived, they attempted to approach Revels' vehicle, and he fatally shot himself, police said. They found a gun next to his body.

Detectives are waiting for a formal coroner's identification, but they believe the dead man is the man wanted in the deadly shooting rampage, according to Yoshida.

Los Angeles County sheriff's detectives went to Revels' home in the 15800 block of Greenrock Avenue in Lancaster on Friday afternoon to check on a woman who lived with him. Inside the home, they found the body of 62-year-old Cornelia McIntosh, who had been shot, investigators said. Yoshida said the killing may have occurred before the other shootings. The investigation is continuing. "What motivated the shootings? We don't know at this point," Yoshida said. "We know he knew all of his victims."

This left me completely traumatized because I started to see the pattern, and how mental health is generational and profoundly serious. Two of the most important men I needed in my life growing up and as an adult where both gone. At that point I was carrying the weight of having lost my dad 18 days before my birthday and my grandad a few months before my wedding, both to suicide, and both to suicide in the same way. After my mom gave me that news I should have went and searched for professional help, but I did not. I was down for a few days, but it was back to planning the wedding. July 9th came, and everything was gorgeous, from the decorations to all our beautiful family that attended, but that day for me was very emotional. I was sad because my mom got food poisoning the night before, so she wasn't her normal self, hurt because neither my father nor his dad was there to walk me down the aisle and happiness all at the same time because this began the start to a new life of fullness for me. It felt and looked like a fairytale beginning.

Now that the wedding is over...I feel like I can speak on this topic because I have been married for four years now. Therefore, I have seen firsthand how childhoods and upbringing play a major part in a person's personality, actions and reactions. My marriage, just like any other, has good days where we are completely in sync, and bad days when leaving feels like the best option. I must be honest... I have always been the one who would throw divorce or separation in the air when I felt like things were too bad to handle. And he would always say, "Say what you mean, and mean what you say." I did not care about that because the men in my life left me when things got hard, so I was okay with that disfunction. Even though we heard what we signed up for; better or worse, rich or poor, sickness and in health, we did not know what that looked like being legally bonded to someone. Being married means that you can't just run when things get hard and you can't just shut your partner out. It's rules to being married and being understanding is a major one that comes with the deal.

The very next day after we got married, I was hit with another wave of emotions, and it was not from the wedding day. My husband's ex, the same ex I caught him conversating with during our dating stage, left him what seemed like a final goodbye love post on Instagram. I was livid. I was in total shock and disbelief, not mainly because of what she did, but because we literally just got married and still, we were dealing with the same problems we had while dating. Speaking up for myself and this new covenant I just agreed to cherish for life, I exchanged words with her...She explained that she was at his bachelor's party, and that my new husband had invited her.

That started the dynamic of our marriage. Well, for me it did. I was supposed to be feeling on top of the world...instead I felt unvalued. I wanted to leave, but I never heard of anyone divorcing the day after they got married. So, just like before I swept it under the rug, but I did not forgive him for anything he put me through, and it showed in the way I talked to him when I would even feel like he was lying to me. I verbally tore him down every chance I got when I would find out about him not being 100% honest about things. It could even be little things he keeps from me and I would blow it up bigger because I did not trust him. I was hurt and I wanted him to feel the same way I felt. I made a promise at the beginning of our relationship that I would always be upfront with him... I did not cheat or start another relationship with anyone else, because I knew that would only give him free will to keep the cycle going, but I wanted him to feel my pain in some form, so verbal abuse is what I gave him.

Because our relationship before marriage had so much distrust, lies, lack of respect, ineffective communication and little examples of strong relationships or marriages, it felt as if we were destined to fail. I have no idea why we thought getting married would make the problems go away, but it did not. If anything, marriage placed a magnifying glass over every issue we had not healed from. The first three years of our marriage were an exact reflection of our dating stage. The only difference now was that we stood before God and all of our family, promising that no matter what we would be together until death do us part. Those vows were the difference. This is why I will stress the fact that it is important to heal before making life changing decisions. Because had we really healed from our pasts, individually, I would not have been trying to find my happiness in him, and vice versa. When this happens it places too much responsibility on one person. I should not have put him on a pedestal to be the one to fill the void my father left me with. I realize now that I placed all of my expectations on him, and when he failed to meet my unspoken or unrealistic expectations, I blamed him, instead of myself.

One year later, it is 2017 and we find out we are pregnant again with our son, Cortland Jaryan Moten, Jr. Honestly, I was in no space mentally, physically, or emotionally to bring another baby into this world. I do not like admitting this, but I thought heavily about abortion... on my own...without my husband's opinion. At that time I did not feel like I had love to give myself, let alone 2 children. My husband reassured me that he would be there with me every step of the way, and now that he is here, I could not imagine life without him. By this time, I am a senior in college, married, a new mom with a baby on my hip and now one on the way. One thing I was determined to do that year was graduate, and despite all of the setbacks and emotional breakdowns, I walked across that stage April 28, 2018 with a Bachelor's Degree in Biology, Pre-Veterinarian. On the outside looking in it may have seemed as if I had it all together because naturally, I am a happy person. Only God and I know how many mental battles I had within myself just to keep going and not give up all while being a full-time student, wife, mother, and employee.

Nobody really stresses the fact that once you have said I do, the wedding is over, the guests and family have gone back to their own lives, and that the work is complete. Wrong! Once the wedding is over, that is when the real work starts. It is only supposed to be you, your partner and God, that is it. Well, the first three years of our marriage it was only me and Cortland. We did not invite God into our union at all and it showed early. Yes, we did pre-marital counseling and we sat there every weekend and smiled in our counselors faces as they repeatedly mentioned how marriage does not work unless God is involved, and that prayer is your battlefield. I would say we did what the bible told us not to do, we went into marriage lightly. We both did not commit to anything dealing with God. We did not commit to the most important things like constant prayer and finding a church home. We needed these ingredients to make our friendship, relationship, and marriage last. We thought all we needed was love and each other. One thing I have realized since being married is that love is not just a feeling, love is an action word. Love is waking up every morning and choosing to put someone else's needs before your own. Love is unconditional. Love is not selfish. Feelings change every minute, but love, real love takes dedication, action and work.

Chapter 7

The Love Ran Out

The love we thought we needed, ran out August 2019. I was completely fed up with my point of view not being understood, fed up with not feeling like we were on the same page with parenting, communication and just everyday life. We had a huge fall out that led to me throwing his clothes in our apartment trash and also throwing my wedding ring out the front door. That night I said things that I knew would cut any man to his core, and at that time I did not care. I threatened to take our kids away from him, and to get a divorce and move back home with my mother. Like I mentioned before, around that time my mom had become my best friend, my favorite person in the whole world and everyone, especially my husband knew I placed her on a higher pedestal than I did him at the time.

Even though I knew it was causing friction in our marriage, I bragged on my mom all the time, and I confided in her about any and everything even before I would come to him sometimes. Once I became a mother, she became my saving grace. I called her every day and told her everything that was going on in my life, and in my eyes, she was everything I needed to survive. Our relationship took a turn for the worse when I started going through problems within my marriage and needed her for support and guidance. She no longer acted like the person I would brag on at the beginning of me and Cortland's relationship. Mentally I was depressed and not wanting to live at all, but I still had faith that if I needed my mom she would definitely come through. I was staying in Jackson, Mississippi with no family or friends...Cortland and I were not on good terms at all so I decided to ask my mom if the kids and I could come stay with her while I mentally get myself together and work so that I could get us our own apartment. She told me no.

At the time I was hurt and confused, but I was not mad at her decision because ultimately that is her house and as an adult with a family of my own, it is not her responsibility to pick up my broken pieces. What did hurt my feelings to the core was when it started to feel like my coming around her was being a bother. She would text and check on Cortland to see how he was doing, but I could be in the same house with her and we would have no conversation of how I was doing mentally. Since she told me I could not stay with her until I got on my feet, I started looking for my own apartment in Memphis, from Jackson. I began to lash out at my mom any chance I got. It was one statement that she made that mentally sent me overboard. She said I did my part raising you all, now it is time for you all to handle life on your own. I say it mentally sent me overboard because I did not feel like she raised us to the point where we could handle life on our own, all I felt that she did was provide and I verbally expressed that in very evil ways that I have had to apologize for. It was already stressful enough going through everything I was going through, so after the first apartments denied me, I stopped looking. A few weeks passed and I found myself apologizing to Cortland and suggesting that we go back to counseling because I honestly did not want our marriage to end. I guess the things I did and said that night affected him more than I thought, because his mind was set on separating. I suggested that he could move out since there was no moving past this in his mind, and he agreed. My depression became severe and I seriously contemplated taking my own life. I felt like my problems where bigger than me and that I could not take it anymore. I entered myself into therapy to keep me from losing my mind. I also did something that I didn't do from the beginning. I tried someone that has always had my life in his hands. I never acknowledged Him or depended on Him but this time...I tried God. I downloaded a bible app and started different bible plans that spoke about my exact situations and how I was feeling. Even on my worst days I would read those plans and write down my feelings instead of keeping them in my head and I started feeling better about the meaning of life one day at a time. That is what stopped my suicidal thoughts and that is why I am here today...Because I tried God!

Now unlike myself, Cortland was able to find a place and was set to move out in December. At that time, I was working at Bath and Body Works and every day when I went to work, I could not help but cry from being overwhelmed with emotions. My manager became a mother figure to me during that time. She gave me encouraging words every day, a raise, and a manager position. She knew I needed it...She also knew my circumstances at home due to me crying every day. She knew I would not be able to handle all of my bills on my own with the checks I had been getting. I started having faith that God was working on my behalf. All of a sudden, my checks started getting garnished from a bank I left in overdraft years ago and at the same time my apartment became infested with bed bugs. I had the smallest breakdown ever. I cried and felt overwhelmed for just a second, then I thought about God and the things I had been reading in my daily plans. One fact about Him stood out to me which was he said that he will never leave nor forsake you. I am a living witness to this statement. Even though I was living paycheck to paycheck, had to get rid of all our furniture, and slept on the floor and an air mattress for months, God made sure all of my bills were paid and we had food every day. This strengthened my faith in Him to the point where now, if I am faced with challenges, I think about the time I thought I wanted my life to end and how His Word changed my perspective. At that moment I knew God took my mother, my husband, my comfort, and my pride from me in order to show me that without Him nothing I have is possible. He met me at my lowest and He changed me, my mindset, and my direction in life. During this storm I saw clearly how we are what we have been through. We are our traumas. It takes courage, but it is up to us as adults to look at ourselves, our flaws, our shortcomings and where our own hurt and pain stems from, and heal, before we can love, understand, and even try to judge anyone else.

To My Mother,

I want to start by saying I love you with everything in me. We have been through a lot, but at the end of the day you have always been right here. You are still here despite all the disrespect and negativity I gave you and I am sorry. You did not leave when things got tough on you and I appreciate that tremendously. Now that I am a mother, I understand that you loved us the best way you knew how. I forgive and have forgiven you for everything and I will love you and cherish you forever. You are my everything.

Love Imani

Chapter 8

Shhh...The Unspoken Truth

The unspoken truth is that nobody wants to share their experiences (especially in the black community) because it will make their parents seem less than God like. God-like as in picture perfect parents who have done nothing wrong or have not contributed to your depression, anxiety and etc. in any kind of way. When in reality, sharing your experiences helps the younger generation and generations to come to understand on a level of respect, what you have made it through, in spite of. Anyone who has experienced having parents of course loves their parents no matter how bad the relationship is or was, but some parents have too much pride to accept the fact that they played a role in the outcome of their adult children lives. Just like their parents played a role in how they dealt with life as an adult. It is generational. Since I have started my healing journey and letting others know my story and why I am so passionate about healing from childhood traumas, I have spoken to many peers around my age and older that have experienced similar or worse traumas than I have. I must say that unhealed traumas are the reason for broken homes, failed marriages and bad communication in general. We must get out of that stagnant mindset that follows us from childhood to adulthood because my mom and dad treated me this way, I will grow up treating others and myself this way or worse. This is what stops our growth, our blessings, and our healing.

I could not see the blessings in being a wife or having children because of the little girl in me that still had not acknowledged all of my traumas. It was not until I started to be honest with myself and God about my own actions and where they stemmed from. My marriage and relationship with my mother also started to heal. During my separation with my husband, we both focused on ourselves, talked to other people and did what made us happy at that time just like two young people who felt like they jumped into a commitment to soon would do. Divorce was constantly being mentioned and we were so close to following through with it, but God alone stepped in. I mean He stepped in and made an entire 360 degree turn around. I saw how my new relationship with God sent blessings I never knew I could receive. I am no longer worried about my finances, and when I looked at myself, my flaws, and my traumas... My relationship with everyone else got better. I gave all that negativity to my Father, God...The one who wants to carry my load. Once my husband and I were able to actually talk to each other with honesty, compassion and understanding for one another, we were able to see why we needed each other and what marriage really means. You see, marriage is God's invention and He intended it to reflect the way He loves us which is unconditionally. Marriage is important and sacred to Him and it should be to us as well. Therefore, He tells us not to go into it lightly. He does not tell us that for His own pleasure, but rather for our own good. We are supposed to know our spouse, and the person we will bear children with because that is the foundation of our legacy. It is unfortunate that many legacies have crumbled due to unhealed traumas and that is the unspoken truth.

I am a living witness that childhood traumas are revolving doors. I say that because in the area of motherhood I have struggled tremendously. I realized that I did not know how to show my children 100% motherly affection. Just like my mother, I have no issues providing their needs and being present, but emotionally I struggled, and it killed me. I went from having no kids to never baby-sitting kids straight to having two kids of my own really quick. I did not realize just how short my patience was until I had kids... And boy did my kids heighted that fact about me. I also became a yeller. My thoughts before I decided to start my healing journey was that this is how I was raised, so there is no harm. I remembered as a child how I felt being yelled at and how it produced so much anger in me that even as an adult I did not know how to have disagreements without talking reckless and yelling. How could I show my children the type of love I never experienced? I could not, not by myself anyway. It is still a daily working progress. It is not easy learning new ways to love others and yourself especially when you are so accustomed to the feeling of negativity. I hope and pray that when my kids grow up, they will read this book and understand that not only is mental health important, but it is also the way of life. How you feel about yourself and how others have made you to feel about yourself is how you will act and treat others...Even your kids if you do not heal.

Chapter 9

Forgiveness

The hardest thing to do also includes forgiving God...Let's be honest...Healing is an ugly, but necessary process, and at some point, we must forgive. We must forgive God, ourselves and those who have done us wrong. Some may question why I say we must forgive God. I say this because speaking from my own experience, there were a lot of times when I questioned why He allowed me to go through the things that I thought where too much for me to bear. In time I grew to understand that He does not need our forgiveness we need His, and His intentions are always pure despite the trials we endure. The more I blamed God and others for my depression, my anxiety, and my feelings of worthlessness, the more I lost myself to the ways of the world. Marijuana became an everyday coping mechanism to ease the pain and constant doubts that I had about myself. This placed me in a state of comfort and marijuana became my peace of mind. I did not think or turn to God as my first option when I was faced with problems. Ultimately, I think that is the reason why I hit rock bottom. I depended on marijuana to numb me about the things I went through or was going through. I am learning that when you place your faith in the things of this world you will always, eventually hit rock bottom. However, when we learn how to start putting our faith in someone we cannot see, it encourages us to hope and pray for better days. Forgiving God is necessary. Some believe that because He allowed us to go through bad times that we can't trust or forgive Him, so in return we hold a grudge towards God and turn a deaf ear to what He says. This type of ignorance will block all of our blessings. God says that everything is working together for our good! Everything we have endured- the good, the bad and the ugly is working together for our good. I would say the first step to healing is forgiving God, because His intentions are never to hurt or harm us, but to help us through our storms and hard times so that He gets the glory when we come out on top.

"Be strong and be brave! Do not be afraid of them, because the Lord your God goes with you. He will never leave nor forget you..."

-Deuteronomy 31:6

Forgive Your Parents

Forgiving our parents is necessary because our parents are human. They have experienced things in their lives as children and young adults that molded them into the parents that they were or were not to you. Since I have started my healing journey and letting others know my story and why I am so passionate about healing from childhood traumas, and traumas in general, talking with those my age and older has helped me realize that as adults we are in some way holding grudges against our parents or others that wronged us in any way. In order to be better than what we have been through we must forgive. One because we are not perfect ourselves and we will also make mistakes in this world and two, because God will not forgive us if we cannot forgive others. When we hold on to that offense or allow it to replay over and over again in our minds, we allow that moment to control our lives. We do not trust others because at some point someone took advantage of our trust. In essence, we do not know how to love unconditionally because we have the mindset of "what are you going to do for me".

Those feelings grow with us, the older we get the more we start to act out on those feelings and emotions. You must take those hard steps towards healing and becoming a better human being for yourself. Talk with your parents about how they treated you as a child and how that made you feel. If you can't do that or if they have passed already, write a letter to them expressing all of your feelings and once you are done burn that letter or throw it away. This is a physical representation of you letting go of the past and moving forward. When my mother and I fell out I realized that I had so much to say that I had not forgiven her for, and all of my actions and reactions were based off of the love I did not feel as a child. In order for me to be a better version of myself I felt like I had to tell her what damaged me as a child, because those things where now guiding my life and the way I saw life to be.

Once I had the courage to finally talk to her without the negativity and disrespect and express my position as a hurt child, I felt like a huge weight had been lifted from my shoulders. She listened to me and understood where my hurt and pain came from and I listened to her and understood how it is also hard from a single parent's perspective. From that point on I knew I could not blame her for my actions as an adult any longer. After that conversation, it did not happen that night, but over time I started to feel in control of my life and the direction I wanted to move in. The little girl inside of me was finding peace through all of the negativity she held on to and ultimately the woman I am now was able to start blossoming.

Forgive Yourself

For me this was the hardest and longest process to accept because mentally we as human beings are harder on ourselves than anyone else. Once you have been accustomed to negativity and negative thoughts it becomes the way you start to view yourself. It seems as if nothing you do is right or enough so that others can see the good in you. This is what the devil wants us to believe about ourselves. He wants us to believe that we need validation from our peers, parents, and partners when in fact, God is the only judgment that matters. When we are so focused on the negative things, we leave no room for God to provide us with the true joy and peace that only He can give. We turn to the things of this world like drugs, constant partying, or knowingly bad relationships to ease our pain and the constant negative thoughts, but in reality, it only numbs you for just a moment. God's peace is eternal, and it is already paid for...All you have to do is ask for His help and He will help you take care of the rest. At the end of the day, we must remember that we are not supposed to be living to be praised here on earth, because it is a guarantee that we will leave from this place. We are supposed to be living in a way that we can be welcomed into Heaven with open arms, because that is where our riches reside. Forgiving yourself may be hard, but it is necessary for our own personal growth in this world and in God.

Chapter 10

Without God, it is Impossible

Without God true healing is impossible! Without God your process will end faster than you think because he did not intend for us to handle the impossible by ourselves. But God! With God everything under the sun is possible. When I was on the verge of taking my life, He loved me more than I loved myself. I was at my lowest...the lowest I have ever felt in my life. If it were not for God, I could not have written this book to tell you how I made it through in spite of everything the devil threw my way. If He can take me, a damaged, used, and abused sinner and change my outlook on this world and the ultimate goal of life, which is to make it to heaven, I know for a fact He can also turn your dark days into light-You just have to give Him a chance. To be completely honest with you, giving Him a chance is hard to do as well and this is only because you have gotten comfortable with your own coping mechanism. It can definitely be hard to give your problems to someone you have never seen or tried. It is hard, but I will say this again, it is necessary! It was necessary that you went through your trials because if you had not you would not be a testimony for others. Through your testimony of survival broken people can have hope and believe that impossible circumstances can change for the better. It was necessary that you hit rock bottom so that you will never want to experience that situation again. If you are reading this you have made it 100% through all of your bad days, and that was not from your own doing. God is not done with you and I pray that you learn to turn to Him in every time of need and not to the things of this world.

I encourage everyone reading this book, if you have not already, to completely give God one problem in your life that you can't seem to stop worrying about. It could be something as small as not having enough money to pay your light bill or something as big as your childhood traumas. Whatever you choose to give Him, completely take your hands off of the situation, ask God for help in that area and watch Him take care of you. He did it for me. God will meet you right where you are in your depression, in your addiction, in your lowest moment. The bible says He loves those who feel weak because He has the opportunity to not only show Himself strong, but to make you strong again. So, no matter what you have endured in your life, no matter how much wrong you have done, no matter how defeated you feel, if you trust Him to change your life and renew your mind, I am confident in saying He will. He met me in my addiction and in my depression and He has done more for me than I could ever do for myself. Your childhood traumas may have evolved into adult mental issues, but if you are still here God is not done with you!

It is time to HEAL!

Your Turn...

Self-Help Healing Journal

Look back over your life and answer the following questions honestly and to the best of your ability. Writing down your traumas, negative, and even positive thoughts on paper helped me to start healing and I am praying the same thing happens for you!

1. If any, list one or more of your childhood traumas.

2. How did you feel, and did you have any help sorting out your emotions and feelings?

3. Did you receive any professional help whether it be from a pastor, therapist, or counselor?

4. Did the trauma(s) and feelings follow you into your adult life?

5. Do you think it is too late to renew your mind from negativity?

6. If any, what are some traumas you have experienced as an adult?

7. In your adult life have you talked with a therapist about the traumas you experienced? If so, how did you feel during and afterwards?

8. How do you respond to those who have wronged you?

9. Have you tried giving one problem to God to see His work?

10. How do you think giving control over your life to someone you have not seen make you feel?

Encouraging Quotes by

Imani Revels-Moten

To better understand people

As I have become more aware of myself and others around me, I understand that everyone has gone through, is going through or will go through a situation that will change them and their outlook on life.

To be more aware of your sin

I am not living to be praised on earth, I am living in a way that I can be welcomed into Heaven.

To strive for dreams while you are alive

You do not know when your time here is done, so while you are here, make an impression.

To stay strong during trails

We have sight, so that what we see should not be what we focus on during our dark times. We should focus on our faith!

To be a blessing to everyone I come in contact with

If I can be a blessing to others, God will continue to flood me with blessings.

About the Author

My name is Imani Revels-Moten. I was born in Colorado, Colorado and raised in Memphis, TN. My parents were not bad parents and they provided and showed love the best way they knew how. At a young age they dealt with childhood traumas and I could tell by the way they handled my siblings and me. Growing up I was molested and raped by my father from the age of 5 until the age of 13. February 10, 2008, he committed suicide. From then on, my younger siblings and I were raised by my mother, who also dealt with pain and traumas, and she always yelled to get her point across. Growing up one thing I noticed about myself was I could forgive quickly. I never hated my father, I wanted to know what happened to him and why he thought having sex with his daughter was okay. Because my childhood confused my definition of what love is, I grew up excepting the bare minimum from relationships. I would put my expectations on others and get mad when they did not live up to it. I am now a mother to two beautiful babies, a wife of four years and a graduate of Jackson State University with a Bachelors in Pre-Veterinary.

I recently had a mental breakdown the end of 2019. My marriage was failing tremendously, and my mother completely left me alone when my husband and I went through our separation. I thought about taking my life, but God. He stepped in right on time and gave me strength. So often we leave our life and happiness in the hands of people who are not capable of keeping us or themselves happy. The only one who is truly capable of giving us a peace that surpasses all understanding is Jesus. God sent Jesus to take the weight off of your shoulders and once I realized that I felt a need to tell my testimony.

We do not have to be how we were treated and we do not have to treat others the way they treated us. Our blessings do not come from this earth nor the people. Our blessings come from someone much stronger and powerful than us and we are to be living examples of Him. You see, if we love as He does, and have complete faith in Him and His Word, when this world is gone, with him is where we belong.

-Imani

ABOUT THE PUBLISHER

Established in 2013, CoolBird Publishing House is a division of CoolBird Studios, LLC and is nestled away in the small quaint town of Goodwater, Alabama. To learn more about CoolBird Publishing House and our services, visit www.coolbirdstudios.com

CoolBird Publishing House
THE AUTHOR'S NEST

www.ingramcontent.com/pod-product-compliance
Lightning Source LLC
LaVergne TN
LVHW020657100826
845148LV00012B/2541

* 9 7 8 0 5 7 8 8 6 2 4 5 3 *